What We Have in Common

A Brim Coloring Book

Written by Jane Landey
Edited by David Austin
Drawings by David Austin and Jane
Austin Copyright©2017

Published by CreateSpace:An Amazon Company.
Printed in U.S.A.

Introduction

What We Have in Common. Brim Coloring Books enable children to color the drawings as they read along! The books display the similarities of related animals. In this series, the camel and the llama are compared. The facts enable children to appreciate common values. Thus, imbibing in them interest towards animals which could help them appreciate what they have in common with one another.

THE CAMEL

AND

THE LLAMA

The camel and the llama have many things in common. They look alike and both carry loads and people on their backs.
Both can survive the Sahara desert.

A camel and a llama meet on a
sunny day on the Sahara.

I am a camel.

I am a llama.

I can carry a huge load.

I can too!

I can carry more than one person on my back!

I can too!

I can walk a long distance.

I can too!

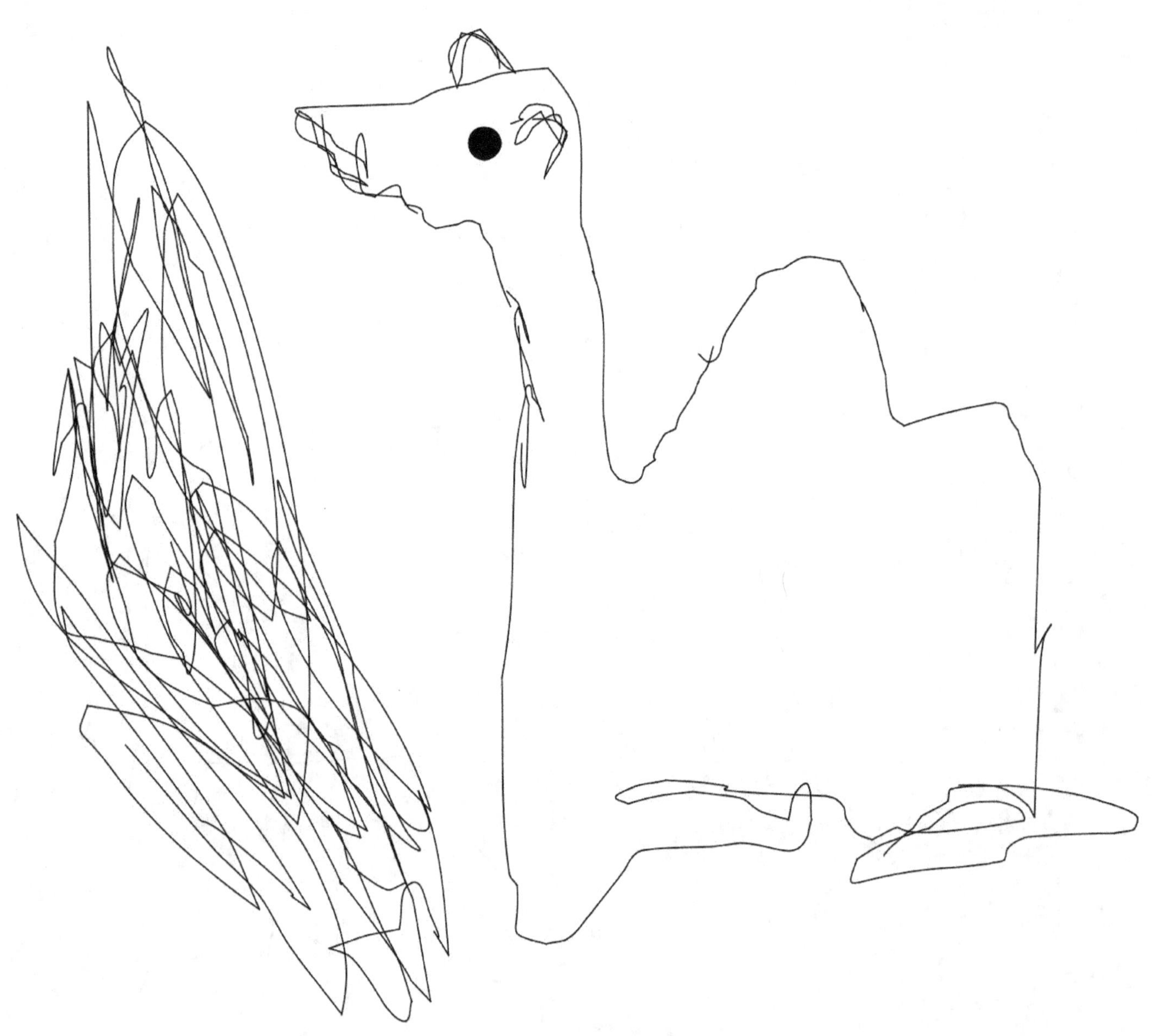

I drink a lot of water and reserve it!

I can too!

I carry people across the desert!

I do carry people across the desert too!

I have a long oblong head.

I have a long oblong head too!

I love to grunt.

Hun, hun,hun!

I love to grunt too!

I can also hiss.

I can hiss too!

I can refuse to move!

I can refuse to move too!

I work hard for my master!

I work hard for my master too!

I graze on grasses!

So do I!

I eat hay too!

So do I!

I carry loads to the market for sale.

Market
So do I!

Sad, I am slaughtered for meat!

Sad, I am slaughtered for meat too!

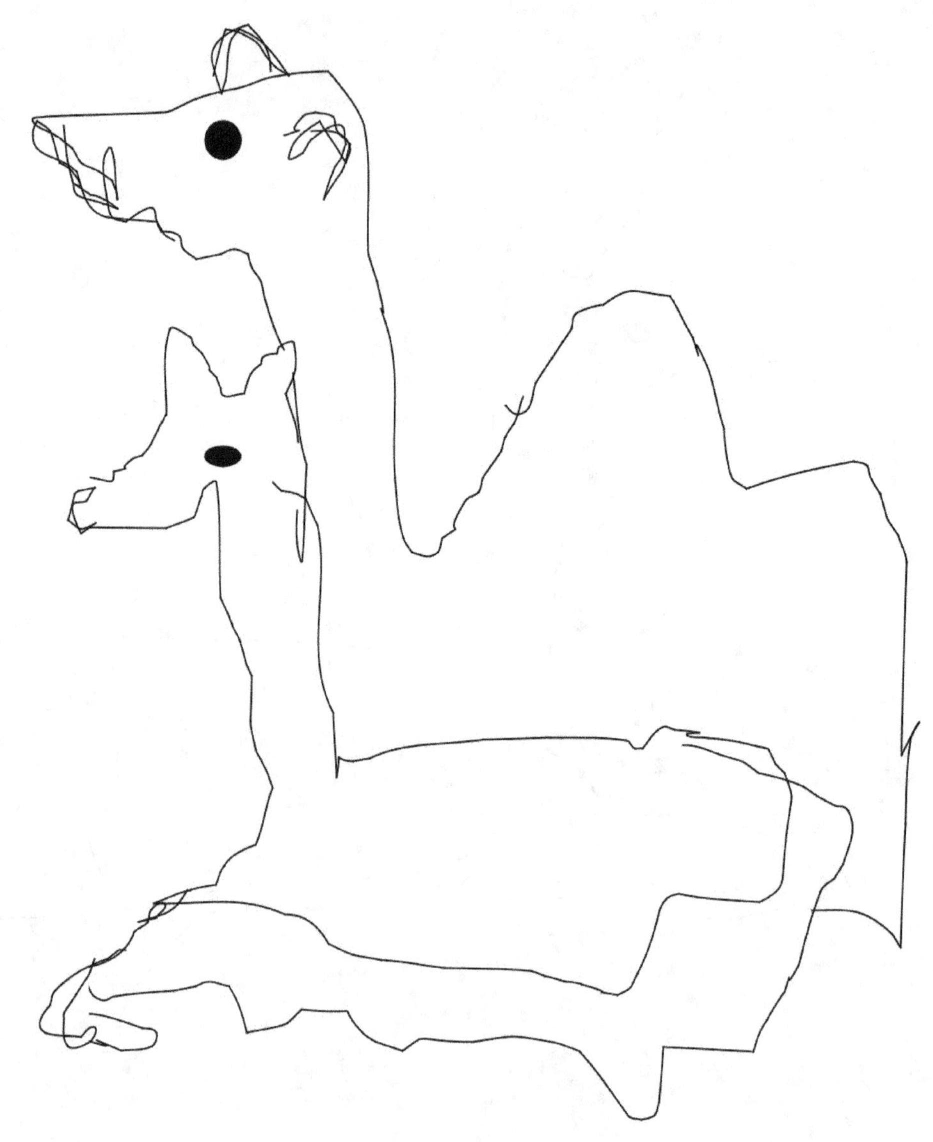

We are both of a kind!

What We Have in Common Brim Coloring Books

Crocodile and Alligator
Turtle and Tortoise
Starfish and Octopus
Worm and Snake
Turkey and Vulture
Ostrich and Emu
Weka and Kiwi
Bat and Rat
Camel and Llama
Duck and Pelican
Kangaroo and Wallaby
Pig and Tapir
Skunk and Squirrel
Hedge and Anteater
Cat and Owl
Elephant and Rhinoceros
Dog and Fox
Buffalo and Bull
Leopard and Cheetah
Horse and Zebra